# CLASSICAL l

## an insid

## by Hugh Hollinghurst

## for the Liverpool History Society
### MMXI

Cover illustrations (*from top to bottom*):
*St George's Great Hall window (see page 7),* Meleager and Atalanta
*(detail) from the studio of Paul Peter Rubens in the Walker Art Gallery
(see page 64) and hydria with Dionysus, Athene, Apollo and Artemis in
the World Museum (see page 87)*

ISBN 978-0-9559428-2-2

Designed and typeset by Peter Owen in Constantia
Cover design by Ron Jones

The Liverpool History Society would like to record their gratitude for generous grants towards the cost of production from an anonymous charity and from the Historical Society of Lancashire and Cheshire.

Photographs by Hugh Hollinghurst (HH), Paul Hollinghurst (PH) and Peter Owen (PO) unless otherwise attributed.

With grateful thanks to Peter Owen for designing and typesetting the text and illustrations, and to my wife Joan who has encouraged and supported me as always in the project, and who has proof read the text.

By the same author:
Gods and Heroes of Ancient Greece
Greeks and Romans
Chesterfield High School: the first twenty five years
St Luke's Church, Great Crosby: 1853-2003
St Michael's Church, Blundellsands; a centenary history
Birth of an Elephant: Audubon in Liverpool 1826
Classical Liverpool: language, sculpture and architecture
John Foster and Sons: Kings of Georgian Liverpool

Printed in England by Joshua Horgan Print Partnership Oxford

# Introduction to Contents

*Classical Liverpool: an inside story* is arranged by buildings, unlike its companion *Classical Liverpool: Language, Sculpture and Architecture* which is organised by subject. These buildings are grouped into zones of the city: cultural (St George's Hall and adjacent buildings), commercial and university. The introduction to the text is based on the Victoria Gallery and Museum (part of the university zone). Within each zone the buildings are arranged so that you may visit them in the order that they appear in the book.

Cross references to pages in *Classical Liverpool: Language, Sculpture and Architecture* are given thus (CL88). There are some pages referred to so often that it could help to be acquainted with them before reading *Classical Liverpool: an inside story*. These concern the Greek and Roman gods most closely associated with Liverpool: Neptune (CL22-3), Mercury (CL28-9) and Minerva (CL30-1); the orders of Greek architecture (CL42-53); and Classical enrichment (CL78-9).

# Contents
*Each entry marked by a page number forms a double page spread.*

## Victoria Building
### War Memorial: Birth of Western civilisation

*They died yet are not dead.* The inscription (in Greek) *ΟΥΔΕ ΤΕΘΝΑΣΙ ΘΑΝΟΝΤΕΣ* on the War Memorial was originally written as the epitaph for the victorious Greeks who had died in the last, decisive battle of the Persian Wars at Plataea in 479 BC. The thought could also apply to all the Greeks of the period who developed the civilisation that we enjoy today. For Western civilisation was born in Greece and its birth would have been stifled if the Greeks had been defeated by the Persians.

*The War Memorial to the 205 members of the University of Liverpool who died in the First World War [PO]*

At the start of the war the Athenians took the lead in defeating the Persians in the battle of Marathon and their political system ('the most extreme democratic government the world has known') survived to point the way for our favoured system of government. The Greek historian Herodotus was inspired and enabled by the victory over the Persians to write his history of the war and become the 'father of history'. Greek drama, both tragedy and comedy, flourished after the staging of Aeschylus' work *The Persians* that celebrated the success of the Greeks; Sophocles, Euripides and Aristophanes built on his foundations. From the proceeds of the wars, the Athenians funded the construction of the Parthenon that set a standard – more than any other building and group of sculptures – to influence the form of architecture and art through two millennia. The early Greek philosophers and scientists had suffered Persian occupation; their pioneering work was preserved to progress to the achievements of Socrates, martyr to the cause of free speech, Plato (to whose works 'all western philosophy is a footnote') and Aristotle ('master of those that know'). Mathematicians built on the work of Pythagoras, advances were made in astronomy, and medical knowledge recorded by the physician Hippocrates who was born in Cos when recently liberated from the Persians (see page 120).

*Crowning the fireplace hood in the main hall: the University coat of arms with the complete motto* haec otia studia fovent *which means* These days of leisure foster learning. *(CL6-7) [PO]*

The capitals of the columns in the hall derive from early medieval or Romanesque examples, themselves derived from an antique Corinthian style (CL50-1).

*left: Capital with an inverted Ionic scroll (CL48-9)*
*right: Capital with Corinthian acanthus and dentil decoration (CL50-1)*
*[both: PO]*

# St George's Hall
## Great Hall: from the balcony: Liverpool

The Hall aims to celebrate the greatness of Liverpool through the magnificence of its design and decoration. In this it succeeds triumphantly through a display of virtuoso and surpassing extravagance, heightening the impression created by the grandeur of the Neo-Classical exterior (CL45, 50, 57, 60, 79, 81). The Neo-Classical style (CL60) emphasises Liverpool's claim to be a vital part of a new empire like that of Rome bringing peace and civilisation to the world. The theme of trade and the sea, source of her prosperity, permeate the presentation of this claim, represented graphically by the appearance of Mercury, Roman god of trade, and Neptune, Roman god of the sea (as all over Liverpool CL22-23, 28-29). Symbolic figures in relief reinforce a message of moral and intellectual aspiration based on Classical tradition. The sumptuousness reflects the growing wealth and ambition of Liverpool – and the nation – at the time of construction, and historically it is a perfect example of contemporary Neo-Classical design and taste.

Wherever you look you are reminded of Liverpool. A Corporation coat of arms with motto and lavish decoration appears in patterned formation on the ceiling six times, more than any other. In case you miss this, the window over the organ depicts Neptune with his trident on one side of a Liver Bird and a Triton blowing his conch (a trumpet made out of a sea shell) on the other. The motto of the Corporation is in dominant position on a grand scale. The pavement too repeats the motto twice and, if you could see the full floor, there are more representations, including arguably the loveliest in the most beautiful setting of all (see opposite below).

The wonderful ceiling strikes the visitor immediately but when the magnificent tiled floor is open to view, it is difficult to choose between the two. However, the floor has been covered by a wood surface since the 1860s, except for special displays, as the tiles were felt to be unsuitable for dancing. It has therefore been kept perfectly pristine, a dazzling sight on the rare occasions it is open for display.

*North window of the Great Hall. The motto of the Corporation of Liverpool* Deus nobis haec otia fecit *means* God has given us these days of leisure *(CL6) [PO]*

*Liverpool Corporation motto on the tiled floor (only visible when the floor is uncovered) [HH]*

## St George's Hall
### Great Hall: from the balcony: ceiling

The ceiling's overall design is based on the tepidarium (warm room) of the baths of the Roman emperor Caracalla in Rome (see pages 110-1) and appropriately the construction is based on a Roman technique of alleviating the weight of the roof by using hollow bricks like amphorae (pointed storage jars, see pages 82-3). It is elaborately and richly embellished with a symbolic pattern of coats of arms and decorative designs. St George of *England* and the dragon in each of the four corners is supported on both sides by *Liverpool*'s coat of arms. These are linked with those of *lancastria (Lancashire)* and surround the royal coat of arms in the centre as if protecting the *monarchy*. The royal coat of arms also marks the centre of the design on the floor as can be appreciated when it is open to view.

*Interior of the Great Hall (inscribed* The Late Mr HL Elmes, *the architect of the Hall) [Courtesy Liverpool Record Office]*

The Liverpool coats of arms on the vault of the ceiling depict Neptune on one side of a Liver Bird and Mercury on the other. The vertical panels that embrace the coats of arms depict the staff of Mercury (the caduceus, entwined by snakes, CL28-9) on one side and, on the other, fasces (axe and rods bound together, Roman symbols of authority,

CL16-7). The axes have been altered to a less forbidding form, without their blades.

*Corporation coat of arms on the ceiling of the Great Hall with symbols of Mercury (left) and fasces (right) [PO]*

Just above the pendent light supports are a series of panels with alternating designs: one of Neptune's trident in the centre flanked by Nereids (CL24-5) playing the lyre, the other of Mercury's head in the centre with sea horses blowing conches (like Tritons, CL26-7).

*Panel with Mercury and sea horses [PH]*

The pendent light supports are modelled on the prows of Greek ships, a motif that is repeated round the top of the chandeliers and an acknowledgement of the debt Liverpool owed to shipping and the sea.

*right: Pendent light support [PO]*

*below: SPQL [PH]*

*opposite page: Chandelier with prows of Greek ships [PH]*

In between the arches (better seen from the pavement below) are roundels with a delightful cartouche of SPQL (SENATUS POPULUSQUE LIVERPUDLIENSIS 'the senate and people of Liverpool') This is adapted from Rome's SPQR (...ROMANUS) used on official Roman documents and buildings in ancient times to the present day.

There is a wealth of symbolism and meaning in the reliefs in Classical style: for an explanation see the floor level perambulation.

The granite columns are in the Greek Corinthian order like the columns of the exterior (CL50-1). When the organ was put in, two columns were made spare. These were erected outside as gateposts but were subjected to derision (nicknamed 'candlesticks') and re-erected at one of the entrances to Sefton Park.

## St George's Hall
### Great Hall: from the balcony: tiled floor

The floor – most likely covered – displays at each end a semicircular frieze with Tritons, Nereids and putti, riding and besporting themselves with dolphins; Neptune's head is in the middle with balancing trident-heads towards the edge of the flanking design (CL22-7). The frieze encloses one of the most delightful designs for the coat of arms of the Corporation of Liverpool (see page 7). This is connected via an intricate spiral design with the very centre of the hall where the frieze is repeated full circle. Inside is a frame reminiscent of the rays of the sun, or, more likely, the sixteen points of the compass to indicate the outreach of Liverpool's shipping. This message is reinforced by the emblems of Mercury, god of commerce, that appear between the points. Then there is a circular wreath in bay leaf garland design (CL79) that was thought in ancient times to be a safeguard against lightning (CL85). This in turn embraces the Royal coat of arms that reflects its counterpart in the ceiling, together giving the decorative design of the whole hall unity and a fitting climax.

*Centre of the Great Hall's floor. The detail on the back cover shows more clearly Mercury's emblems: a winged helmet surmounting a caduceus (see pages 8-9 and CL28-9). [PO]*

*Frieze (top to bottom): left hand edge (putti riding dolphins, and trident); left centre (Triton and Nereid); centre (Neptune's head) [HH] The right hand half of the frieze is a mirror image of the left.*

## St George's Hall
### Great Hall: floor level: Latin inscriptions and the cardinal virtues

In addition to the breathtaking beauty and grandeur of the hall's lavishly decorated ceiling and floor, there is a complicated and inspiring message in the inscriptions on the pavement. The inscriptions are reinforced by the winged allegories in relief above. These appear in duplicate opposite each other in the corners and spandrels (curved triangular spaces between the arches, see page 8) and are loosely derived from Raphael's frescoes in the Stanza della Segnatura in the Vatican in Rome. They consist of personifications of the Arts, Science and the four cardinal virtues (Justice, Prudence, Temperance and Fortitude). These virtues, and above all justice, were first defined by Plato (see page 4) in his philosophical work *The Republic* as characteristic of the ideal society. The Latin inscriptions relating to these are allied to corresponding ones in English, taken from the Bible, on the other side of the decorative designs on the pavement. It is best to observe the statues as well on this perambulation, although the only one of Classical interest is, uncharacteristically, George Stephenson, near the end of the circuit.

*The perambulation starts at the opposite end to the organ on the right hand side (the south eastern corner) and proceeds anti-clockwise. On the left of the pavement backing on to the Crown Court is the inscription*

LIBERTATIS HONOS ET SCEPTRI JURA DECORI 'the honour of freedom and the rights of the sceptre [are] a glory'. The worn condition shows the wisdom of protecting the main floor from damage with the wooden covering.

*Worn inscription NULLUM ... (see page 15) [HH]*

The grand entrance to the Crown Court is flanked by Ionic columns and pilasters (CL46-49, 73). The capitals of these have, most unusually, a female head between the Ionic scrolls, particularly decorative on the pilasters; the same figure also appears on a decorative device between the pillars, and on the capitals of the pillars, in the Crown Court (illustrated on page 26). She seems to have the crest of a helmet on the back of her head, like Minerva goddess of war (CL30). However, Minerva also has the attribute of wisdom and crafts and her work is often characterised by settling disputes with peaceful outcomes. So she could represent justice in spite of the fact that one of her best known acts displays judgement conspicuous for its savage punishment in a fit of petulant jealousy (see page 116).

*On the left backing on to the corridor is the inscription which draws our attention to the relief in the corner above, illustrating* **Prudence**:

NULLUM NUMEN ABEST IS SIT PRUDENTIA 'a protecting deity is not far away if there were prudence'. IS should be SI: the letters are formed from individual tiles and could have been put back in the wrong order after restoration as some tiles are extremely worn. There is another misplaced tile after SIT. The spot is a word divider and not needed there as patterning separates SIT from PRUDENTIA. But the tile *is* needed between NUMEN and ABEST (see opposite). Note that an asterisk is not inserted after SIT as the quotation is continued (see page 18).

*Misplaced tile [HH]*

## St George's Hall
### Great Hall: floor level: Prudence and Fortitude

The personification of **Prudence** in the corner above is the first of the four cardinal virtues that you meet. Like all the other figures she is portrayed with wings giving her an ethereal, angelic quality but like them has her feet firmly on the ground as well. A putto (CL34) brandishes a torch representing the knowledge that she will find useful, and helps to hold a mirror up to her. With this she can look at herself, indicating that self-knowledge is one of her attributes. *Know Thyself* (γνωθι σεαυτον), inscribed at the entrance to the premier Greek oracle of Apollo at Delphi, was a key maxim for the Greeks. Using her mirror Prudence can look behind herself, and she also has a male mask at the back of her head, showing that she can see causes and effects simultaneously. She rests her left hand on a rock as a sign of the security her virtue can give.

*Prudence [PO]*

*The theme of the four virtues is continued in the next quotation, and relief above, applying to Fortitude:*

TU NE CEDE MALIS SED CONTRA AUDENTIOR ITO 'do not give way to affliction but on the contrary go forward the more boldly'. This is the warning and encouragement given by a priestess to the Roman hero Aeneas on his way down to the underworld in Virgil's epic poem the *Aeneid* (book 6, line 95; CL8). The figure above wears helmet and breastplate as an indication of bravery in war, also emphasised by the lion and the oak tree. She is crowned with the an oak leaf garland, traditionally awarded to a Roman soldier who had saved a citizen's life in battle (CL 85). The putto appears to be drawing attention to the garland and clutching some leaves that maybe he has mischievously snatched for play.

*Fortitude [PO]*

## St George's Hall
### Great Hall: floor level: Science and the Arts

*We now come to the first of the two central inscriptions on a different theme,* **Science**:

*Science inscription. Asterisks mark the beginning and end of a quotation. [HH]*

FELIX QUI POTUIT RERUM COGNOSCERE CAUSAS 'happy is he who has been able to find out the causes of things'. These words (from the Roman poet Virgil again) seem to refer to another Roman poet Lucretius who wrote a poem explaining the philosophy of Epicurus. This was based on the theories of the Greek philosopher Democritus who developed an atomic theory to explain the physical universe. The passage from which the quotation is taken occurs in Virgil's *Georgics* (book 2, line 490). This is a poem on country life and it might seem odd that it contains such a thought. However, the passage continues 'happy too is the man who is friends with the country gods [and has nothing to do with politics and sophisticated city life]'. The figure in the relief above it with her circlet of stars is probably the personification of astronomy. She is accompanied by a representation of the multi-breasted image of the goddess Artemis (Diana) at Ephesus, the traditional attribute of Science. The putti hold globes in their arms, and the figure points both up to the sky and down to the earth indicating the all-embracing scope of science.

*Following on to the next inscription, and relief above it, making a neat pairing with Science is* **The Arts**:

ARS OPERUM INVENTRIX NATURAEQUE AEMULA PROLES 'Art the inventor of works and the rival offspring of nature' (the west-side version has the inexplicable OPERUH). In the relief above, the putti wave blank inscription tablets; the figure, crowned with a laurel wreath as if she has won a competition in an arts festival, holds a book standing for literature, and a lyre for poetry and music. The mask represents drama (see page 118). Masks were worn on stage in Greek plays to give clarity to an actor's image. This could be miniscule particularly for those at the rear of a theatre that could hold 15,000 spectators or more. There is no evidence that the mask was designed to act as a megaphone. The acoustics at a Greek theatre were perfect.

*Science (above) and The Arts (below) [PO]*

*The theme of the four virtues is resumed in the next inscription applying to* **Justice**:

DISCITE JUSTITIAM MONITI ET NON TEMNERE DIVOS: 'learn justice and not to scorn the gods'. This warning is forever spoken by Phlegyas ('fiery') as he is punished in the Underworld. His crime was one of sacrilege: setting fire to Apollo's temple in Delphi. Phlegyas (a Lapith, see page 37) was enraged with him because he had been responsible for the death of his daughter (Coronis, see pages 46-7). Once again the Latin words are those of the Roman epic poet Virgil when describing Aeneas' descent to the underworld. There he finds Phlegyas 'most pitiful of all' being tormented for his wrongdoing and warning everyone to keep to the law (*Aeneid*, book 6 line 620). In the relief above, the personification of Justice holds a sword in one hand and in the other a pair of scales, a symbol of fair punishment in ancient times, going back as far back as Homer's *Iliad*, the earliest work of Greek literature (CL36). She wears a coronet as symbol of authority; one of the putti balances a weighing bowl and the other holds a blank inscription tablet (to record the verdict?).

*Justice [PO]*

*There is no inscription at this point relating to **Temperance**, the relief above in the last corner on the right hand side of the organ. You will however see one later when you come to its counterpart in the corner diagonally opposite. (see pages 24-5)*

In ancient Greek and Roman times the tempo of the party was dictated by an arbiter who regulated how far the wine should be diluted by mixing it in a crater (mixing bowl, see pages 88-9. Here Temperance has extracted the diluted wine from a crater by using an oinochoe (wine pourer) to fill a skyphos (drinking mug). A putto is, like a little child, 'helping' the process but humorously trying to tip the oinochoe the more and thus increase the licentiousness of the party. Only the firm, resisting hand of Temperance restrains him. Instead of a skyphos, at less sober parties a kylix might be used, a wider, shallow cup with a picture on the bottom. Revellers would reveal the picture and play 'kottabos', competing to flick the dregs at a target.

*Temperance [PO]*

*In the two corner triangles on each side of the organ is the motto of the city:* DEUS NOBIS HAEC OTIA FECIT 'God has given us these days of leisure' (CL6).

*On the right hand side of the organ and repeated on the left, appropriately next to the Small Concert Room, is an inscription praising the effect of music:*

FORTIA FACTA MONET CURARUM ET DULCE LEVAMEN 'It encourages brave deeds and pleasant alleviation of cares' (an amalgam of phrases from Virgil's *Aeneid*).

# St George's Hall
## Great Hall: floor level: Hercules and George Stephenson

The two columns on the end of the arcade underneath the organ are in the form of Atlantes (CL74), in the guise of Hercules with the skin of the Nemean lion on his back (see page 92). Ingeniously, the lion's paws cover the join between the male torso and the architectural base. The other columns have capitals decorated with scrolls in a free interpretation of the Greek Ionic order (CL48-9).

*The reliefs are repeated opposite and so will appear in reverse order as you go round on the other side of the hall, together with the Latin inscriptions (except for that of Prudence). So you have a second chance to view them as you return to the other end, and you also have the opportunity to view the ones you have already seen at a more comfortable angle.*

*Hercules [HH]*

*Statue of George Stephenson [HH]*

The last statue before you come to the southwest door is that of George Stephenson. It is the only one in Classical style – surprisingly – because, of all the eminent men featured, he was probably the only one who had not received a Classical education or used it in his working, social or leisure life. It is the earliest statue in the hall, by John Gibson, who specialised in the Classical style in vogue at the time (see pages 40-1); indeed he said that he had modelled the pose on Archimedes, the Greek scientist, engineer, mathematician and inventor. In Roman fashion he wears a toga, a large woollen cloak which would normally have been draped over his left shoulder, but as he is working he has laid it aside (see page 101). Underneath he has a Roman style tunic and wears Roman sandals, not shoes or boots which he would have used for office work or in the field. He holds a drawing board and pair of compasses. Paper and pen would have been anachronistic but they look like what a Roman would use: a wax tablet and pointed stilus to scratch his designs.

## St George's Hall
### Great Hall: floor level: plinths and doors

The plinths for the statues on each side of the central doorways are full of Classical detail. From top to bottom: egg and dart moulding (CL78), tiny triglyphs (CL44, 46) and Erechtheion scrolls (CL80). Underneath, shells remind you of Liverpool's debt to the sea.

Neptune's trident weaves through the intricate tracery of the doors from top to bottom. In the centre is the head of Mercury and above it the legend SPQL (see page 10).

*As you leave the hall by the south west door, your attention is drawn to Temperance again in the corner above by the words* NE

*above: Statue plinths*
*below: NE QUID NIMIS [both HH]*

QUID NIMIS 'don't [do] anything too much' *at the end of the of the pavement design. 'Nothing too much' (μηδεν αγαν) appeared at the entrance to the temple of the oracle of Apollo at Delphi, as 'know thyself' is implied in the personification of Prudence above (see page 16).*

*Upper half of doorway [HH]*

# St George's Hall
## Crown Court: design for justice

The Crown Court is designed to clothe the course of justice with an air of dignity, authority and awe. The Classical style enhances this by creating a scene that gives the impression of palace, throne and temple.

The vaulted roof is dignified by a discreetly decorated ceiling. This is supported by columns in the Corinthian order that match those of the Great Hall in colour and scale, but they have special capitals that are repeated in those flanking the main entrance from the Great Hall (see page 15).

*left: Crown Court pilasters and column [PO]*

*right: Crown Court capital with Minerva (Athene) [PO]*

*Judge's entrance and seat [PO]*

Within this palatial setting the focus of the court is centred on the seat of the judge like a throne. Behind it is a perfect example of an Erechtheion type doorway (CL80) through which he would have entered. The sense of authority this gives is reinforced by two further frames in similar style which are surmounted by a matching pediment with appropriate Classical adornment. The Greek temple atmosphere might engender feelings of religious awe.

The Civil Court (not normally open to the public) balances the Crown Court at the other end of the Great Hall but its intended entrance was hidden by the organ. The design is a mirror image of the Crown Court with minor variations.

## St George's Hall
### North Entrance Hallway: Caryatids and the Parthenon

At Caryae in southern Greece there was a temple dedicated to Artemis. During a festival held in her honour girls would dance holding baskets on their heads (CL74-5). Known as Caryatid maidens, they might also be shown as columns holding up a roof on their heads. There are two freestanding versions of the figures in the north entrance hallway.

Opposite the Parthenon on the Acropolis in Athens is the temple of Erechtheus, called the Erechtheion, and the porch is graced by a row of the six original Caryatids or their copies. The order of architecture of the Parthenon is Doric, the same as the columns that support the north entrance to St George's Hall, so both here and on the Acropolis you have the delightful contrast between the straight, severe masculine Doric style and the flowing, graceful feminine Caryatids (see page 39 and CL42, 75).

Behind the Caryatids and columns, there is a frieze based on that of the Parthenon (a number of casts of the originals are on display in the sculpture gallery of the Walker Art Gallery, see pages 34-6).

*Panel modelled on Parthenon frieze: parade of cavalry. Note the Greek key and ovolo decoration (CL78-9) [HH]*

*left: Caryatid*
*right: Doric columns. The frieze can be seen behind the left hand column. A detail of the decoration of the capital will be found on page 33. [both HH]*

## St George's Hall
### Small Concert Room: Caryatids, ceiling and chandelier

One of the many glories of the Small Concert Room, perhaps the most beautiful interior of the early Victorian period, is the galaxy of Caryatids, possibly more graceful than any others. Their secret is that they only *appear* to support the balcony, and can afford to be slim. In fact they are made of an unknown weak material and the balcony must be cantilevered out from the wall (no drawings of the architect Charles Cockerell survive).

They are in the guise of Flora (goddess of spring and flowers) and Pomona (goddess of fruit and gardens), and they alternate, inclined to left or right.

*Small Concert Room*
*left: Caryatid*
*opposite above: Ceiling*
*opposite below: Chandelier*
*[all HH]*

# St George's Hall
## Small Concert Room: Classical enrichment

*Looking to the back of the stage with the lavishly ornamented Corinthian columns (CL50-1). In the mirrors are reflected the frieze, the chandelier and the dome, perhaps modelled on the caldarium (hot room) of the baths of the emperor Caracalla in Rome, although it is in fact flat and the dome effect only achieved through optical illusion. [HH]*

In the frieze, griffins stand with alternate images of Apollo and his musical instrument, the lyre (see page 117).

*Apollo's lyre surrounded by a proliferation of Classical embellishment:
ovolo, Greek key, garland and Erechtheion scroll, almost a complete
textbook! [HH]*

*Detail of capital in the entrance hall (see page 29) [HH]*

# Walker Art Gallery
## Sculpture Gallery: Parthenon frieze

*In general, Greek names of gods and goddesses are used in works in the Sculpture Gallery, and Roman names in the Picture Gallery (see page 129).*

As you enter the Walker, turn right into the sculpture gallery. Look high up to the left at the frieze on the wall. It is a copy of one that used to adorn the Parthenon (*the temple of the maiden goddess*) in Athens portraying the festival that took place every four years in honour of Athene, the city's patron goddess. The outstanding event of the festival was a ceremonial procession that escorted a newly woven robe to be draped on her ancient statue. The original complete frieze was 150m long and showed a cavalcade of cavalry and chariots processing from each side towards a feast of the gods in the centre who are imagined as being present at the unveiling of the robe.

Only a small selection of the panels that made up the frieze are displayed but they give some idea of the whole ceremony. Starting from the left of the long wall opposite the windows, the first two panels show the parade of cavalry headed by a man who has arrived at the feast of the gods.

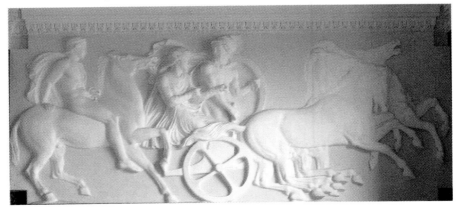

*Parade from the left: from a panel in St George's Hall modelled on the Parthenon frieze (see page 28) [HH]*

The first god to be seen on the third panel is Hermes, messenger of the gods, dressed ready for the road with boots, cloak and broad-brimmed hat. Dionysus, relaxed in his role as god of wine, leans nonchalantly on his shoulder. The corn goddess Demeter comes next holding a long torch as her attribute and touching her chin with her right hand – a conventional sign of mourning in the ancient world – grieving for her daughter Persephone who was carried off by Hades, god of the underworld. Beside her is Ares, god of war, restlessly expressing his fiery temper.

Iris, female messenger of the gods (or the goddess of Victory) can be recognised by her wings and she is accompanied by Hera, queen of the gods, holding up a bridal veil as goddess of marriage. Zeus, king of the gods, sits uniquely on a throne with back and arm rests as the climax to this half of the festival parade. After two humans carrying stools as an invitation to the gods to join in the feast, the feast of the gods continues. Athene, the figurehead and the climax of the festival that is held in her honour, looks at the other half of the procession. She has laid aside her helmet, and her aegis (warrior's cloak) lies on her lap, so she appears in her role of goddess of wisdom and craft, not of war (see pages 15, 82 and CL30-1). Hephaestus turns to speak to her, strong in shoulder and body as befits the blacksmith of the gods. However, a slight distortion of his ankles and the stick beneath his arm hint at the tradition that he was a cripple, thrown out of heaven by Zeus for siding with Hera in a quarrel against him.

*Panel in St George's Hall modelled on Parthenon frieze (see page 28) as described above. From left to right: Iris (with wings), Hera (with veil), Zeus (with beard), Athene, Hephaestus and assistant to priestess. In this version the two humans carrying stools have been omitted. [HH]*

In the original full form of the frieze Apollo, Artemis, Poseidon, Aphrodite and Eros are shown as well. We see the procession advancing towards them with a lively parade of cavalry and chariots echoing the one on the left.

*Panel modelled on Parthenon frieze: parade of cavalry [HH]*

The frieze ran round the top of the inside wall of the colonnade of the temple at a height of 12m (at least four times their hanging position in the Walker). So, to obtain a view of the whole uninterrupted by columns you would have to stand only a few feet away from the inside wall, because of the narrow space between it and the columns, with a very restricted upward field of vision and in poor light. Compare that with the ease of viewing in the gallery now!

Starting on the far left hand wall of the room and continuing round to near the entrance door wall is another frieze, from the temple of Bassae, depicting the battle between the Lapiths and Centaurs. The king of the Lapiths invited his cousins, the Centaurs, to his marriage. Centaurs were half man, half horse, and so unused to wine. They became so drunk that they tried to carry off the bride, women and boys but were driven off in the struggle that ensued.

Battle of Lapiths and Centaurs *from the temple of Bassae*
*[courtesy National Museums Liverpool]*

Near the doorway a block showing a chariot drawn by two deer starts a new sequence in the frieze. It shows a battle between the Greeks and women warriors, the Amazons, and these sculptures continue on the wall above the entrance door.

*opposite: North front of the Parthenon in about 1830. The position of the frieze may be partly seen on the top of the inside wall.*
*This engraving and those on pages 38-39 are taken from* Greece: pictorial, descriptive and historical *by Christopher Wordsworth, 1844.*

## Walker Art Gallery
### Sculpture Gallery: sculptures of Bassae; the Elgin Marbles

The two casts on display on either side of the doorway are different in scale and shape from the others. This is because they are copies of the metopes that decorated the outside of the temple above the columns between the triglyphs so you may stand back as far as you like to view each of these! Their theme is also the battle of the Lapiths and Centaurs but portray individual combats rather than a general melee. This is because the spaces available for the sculptor are separated from each other and squarer in shape whereas the frieze forms a continuous narrative. They are in very high relief (or, putting it another way, much more deeply cut) than the Parthenon and for that reason have even been considered superior to them.

*Reconstruction of the temple of Bassae. The metopes are above the columns on the outside wall between the grooved dividers (triglyphs, CL44, 46)*

The originals of these sculptures adorned the temple of Bassae in southern Greece. They were discovered by John Foster Junior, a Liverpool architect, who toured Greece during the Napoleonic wars when a Grand Tour of Italy was impossible because of the difficulty of travelling through hostile France. He, together with Charles Cockerell (see pages 30 and CL58) and others, was instrumental in securing the sculptures for Britain in the face of competition from France and Germany. In the early 1820s John Foster presented plaster cast copies to the Liverpool Royal Institution in Colquit Street which were later transferred to the Walker Art Gallery.

At the same time as John Foster Junior's expedition to Greece, sculptures from the Parthenon on the Acropolis in Athens were being removed by Lord Elgin, subsequently finding a home in the British Museum and known as the Elgin Marbles. These are the casts on display here, presented to the Liverpool Royal Institution by George IV in 1821. This was probably in recognition of the service that John Foster had rendered in obtaining the statuary of Bassae for Britain. The Parthenon statuary and reliefs were considered to be among the masterpieces of classical sculpture and influenced the work of many 19th century artists. Local sculptors such as BE Spence, who was a student at Liverpool Academy in the 1830s, and an assistant of John Gibson (see page 40), would almost certainly have studied the casts at the Royal Institution which now reside here.

*The corner of the Doric Parthenon is on the right and the Caryatid porch of the Ionic Erechtheion on the left (see page 28). The doorway, archetype for myriads of others (CL80-1), is off the picture to the left.*

*The Tinted Venus* Triumphant and proud, Venus holds a golden apple with the Greek inscription *Η ΚΑΛΗ ΛΑΒΕΤΩ* 'Let the fair one take it'. She has just won the first and most selective beauty contest of all, in which the contestants were herself, Juno and Minerva. The goddess of strife, disliked by the gods and never invited to their feasts, had burst into a marriage banquet attended by all the gods and thrown the apple down into their midst. With Juno, Minerva and Venus each claiming the honour for herself, the argument was resolved by the judgement of Paris who, tempted by the bribe of the most beautiful wife, awarded the apple to Venus. Now, she will arrange for Paris to seduce Helen, wife of Menelaus, King of Sparta in Greece, and carry her off to Troy. So the goddess of strife will be delighted to cause the Trojan War when Greece mounted an expedition to Troy to win her back and the war lasted for ten years. Homer's *Iliad* describes part of the war (Troy was called Ilium by the Greeks) and his *Odyssey* the homecoming of the Greek Odysseus. Together they emerged as the first flowering of Greek literature often referred to as the *Bible of the Greeks*.

John Gibson's statue was controversial as he tinted the statue flesh colour, and highlighted other parts in colour, claiming – rightly – that the ancient Greeks coloured their statuary, as they did their temples. He playfully signed the statue in Greek on the tortoise's carapace using the formula of Greek vase painters *ΓΙΒΣΟΝ ΕΠΟΙΕΙ ΕΝ ΡΩΜΗ* 'Gibson was making (me) in Rome'.

*opposite:* The Tinted Venus *by John Gibson*
*[courtesy National Museums Liverpool]*

*The Death of Verginia* (by Giacomo De Maria) The centrepiece statue in the entrance hall portrays a father supporting the lifeless body of his daughter with one arm and with the other triumphantly raising the blood stained sword he has used to kill her. The reason for this atrocious deed is not apparent as the inscription below is, at the time of writing, incomprehensible to most, incorrect and illegible. The action took place in Rome in 450 BC. The ordinary people (plebs) had fought the aristocracy (patricians) for a set of laws that would safeguard themselves and their freedom. The constitution was suspended and a commission of ten men was chosen to agree laws which became the Twelve Tables, the Roman equivalent of the Ten Commandments. However, the commission, led by Appius Claudius, started a reign of terror that began with the assassination of a political opponent and ended with his lust for a schoolgirl. The beautiful and principled Verginia was already betrothed and Appius failed in his attempts to pressure her to submit to him. Her mother had died, and Appius chose his moment to pounce when her father Verginius was away on active service. Using his official position, he prevailed on a friend to claim that Verginia had been his slave: she had been stolen from his house where she was born, and palmed off on Verginius as his daughter. As she made her way to school the unsuspecting and terrified girl was arrested in one of the tents in the forum. Friends immediately set out to warn her father who only managed to return to Rome in time because Appius' orders for him to remain in post arrived too late. The matter went to trial with Appius himself presiding. He pronounced that his friend's claim on Verginia was lawful: she should become his slave. Her father, seeing that his daughter was bound to fall into Appius' clutches, killed her with the words 'Appius, with this blood I condemn you and your head (= life) to destruction'. Her death was not in vain; the people resisted the arrest of Verginius; Appius was forced into exile and the rights of the people restored.

Maybe Verginius had already decided beforehand what to do to save his daughter from Appius' lust. We are told that he entered the forum on that fateful day shabbily dressed as if for mourning. He does however wear his centurion's helmet. The statue shows the moment when Verginius has just pierced his daughter's body and looks to his sword saying 'with this blood'. He is full of life and vigour, she limp and lifeless. But it is a moment of ultimate sacrifice for freedom, and its triumph in the face of oppression and injustice.

The Latin inscription records the words of Livy, the Roman Historian (book 3, chapter 48) describing the event. It reads 'TE APII TUUMQ E CAPUT SANGUINE HOC CONSECRO'; it should be 'TE APPI TUUMQUE ...'

The door at the back of the entrance hall is a fine example of the Erechtheion type (CL80).

*Erechtheion type doorway [HH]*

# Walker Art Gallery
## Entrance Hall: architecture

The entrance hall is an architectural feast in the Classical style. In addition to the doorway, the Classical decoration and detail are brilliantly highlighted by being picked out in colour as the ancients did. Unfortunately, their colours of red and blue have been worn away on the buildings that survive and only the slightest traces remain in parts, but the gold employed at the Walker is an excellent alternative. One combination has alternate anthemion and palmette decoration surmounted by a thin band with triglyph indentation superimposed by egg and dart (ovolo) embellishment (CL44, 46, 48-9). The cross beams have guttae and squared capitals above them (CL46).

*Anthemion and palmette decoration, triglyph indentation, egg and dart embellishment, guttae and squared capitals [HH]*

Another combination adds variety with small rosettes on the capitals and a larger variety, complementing them, on the 'metopes' between fully fledged triglyphs (CL44-5).

*Rosettes, triglyphs and metopes [HH]*

A third combination on the upper floor of the entrance hall inclines towards the Ionic with scrolls and ornate floral decoration. Again on the upper floor towards the windows there is a Composite version: Ionic scroll combined with Corinthian acanthus (CL53).

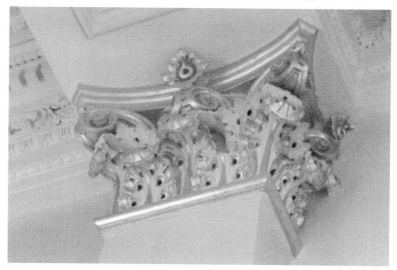

*Composite capital [HH]*

# Walker Art Gallery
## Picture Gallery: Aesculapius, Apollo, and Coronis

*The tour of the Picture Galleries can be followed in order from room to room shown thus [room number], going round in a clockwise direction to the left as you enter, except where indicated.*

***The finding of Aesculapius*** [Entrance Hall] A helpless baby, attended by a goat and a dog, has been discovered by a shepherd. He is amazed and delighted by his find but his manner also suggests reverence as the child is bathed in holy light. The shepherd had been looking for some missing animals but found an infant being suckled by a nanny goat and guarded by a dog. He had been exposed on the hillside by Coronis, the lover of Apollo, father of the child, and he grew up to be Aesculapius, also a god of healing. The light indicates Zeus' blessing and the serpent foreshadows Aesculapius' emblem.

Two other versions of this fascinating myth are described by the Greek travel writer Pausanias who wrote *A Guide to Greece* in the second century AD (Book 1, chapter 26). He says he does not believe one of these as it is discredited by one of the oracles of the priestess (of Apollo!) at Delphi.

***Apollo and Coronis*** [seen later in Room 4] Coronis lies in a deep sleep. Surprisingly, and ironically, the shadowy figure picking herbs is Apollo, the god of healing, light and the sun. He is desperately trying to heal his dying lover who had become pregnant, then unfaithful to him. When he complained to his sister, the virgin and huntress goddess Diana, she caused Coronis to fall into a coma that would end in her death. It was as if Diana in her spite had shot a quiverful of arrows at her. Apollo was filled with remorse, but to no avail. The funeral pyre is already being prepared for the corpse, and bystanders, including Cupid, the god of love (just to the right of Apollo's head), are in mourning. Coronis, her raiment and the flowers contrast with the encircling gloom – except for the sky that irradiates her. And there is a glimmer of light reflected from the heavens on the water: Mercury saved the baby by cutting him from Coronis' womb and appropriately he became the god of healing, Asclepius. But the anger and grief of Coronis' father Phlegyas ended in tragedy (see page 20).

The finding of Aesculapius *by Giovanni Tognolli [courtesy National Museums Liverpool]*

Apollo and Coronis *by Adam Elsheimer (one of the smallest paintings in the gallery) [courtesy National Museums Liverpool]*

# Walker Art Gallery
Picture Gallery: Perseus and Andromeda

Three Classical gods stand out in the public sculpture of the city: Neptune god of the sea, Mercury god of commerce and Minerva goddess of wisdom and the arts (CL22-3, 28-9, 30-1). All of them also feature in works at the Walker Art Gallery.

***Perseus and Andromeda*** [room 8] Andromeda is struggling to free herself from the grip of a sea monster. Her clothes are slipping off; she is looking up desperately for rescue; the fire breathing monster, struck by an arrow, is also looking up, and can see what she cannot: its assailant. For her rescuer, bathed in light, has arrived on a winged horse. Their radiance contrasts with the dark of the monster and the surrounding rocks but complements the luminescence of Andromeda's body.

Andromeda's mother, Queen Cassiopeia, had boasted that she and her daughter were more beautiful than the Nereids (mermaids). When they complained of the insult to their protector Neptune, he sent a sea monster to devastate the territory round Joppa in Ethiopia. King Cepheus, on consulting an oracle, was told he must sacrifice Andromeda to the monster to stop the devastation. She was chained to a rock but Perseus flew by on the winged horse Pegasus. Falling in love with her at first sight, he approached the King and Queen and made an agreement that he would rescue Andromeda if they agreed to his marrying her. Perseus has arrived just at the critical and dramatic point when the monster is about to devour its victim. Perseus killed the monster, rescued Andromeda and claimed her as his bride. But at the wedding feast Cepheus and Cassiopeia reneged on their promise. In the ensuing argument and fight, Perseus was forced to show the Gorgon's head that he was carrying which turned them to stone (see also pages 84 and 100, and CL38).

*opposite:* Perseus and Andromeda *by Frederic Leighton. The picture is framed by two finely wrought gilded Ionic columns. [courtesy National Museums Liverpool]*

## Walker Art Gallery
### Picture Gallery: Europa; Orpheus

***The Rape of Europa*** [room 8] As she is taken away to sea, Europa looks back desperately towards the land. Zeus had fallen in love with her but was afraid of Hera's jealousy and changed himself into a bull to secretly satisfy his desire. The bull has an expectant and knowing look in his eyes as he carries Europa off from Phoenicia in Asia to Crete. There she will have a son, King Minos, and give her name to the continent she reaches.

The Rape of Europa *by George Frederic Watts [courtesy National Museums Liverpool]*

***The Rape of Europa*** In another version [seen later in room 3] a party is enlivened by girls joyously weaving garlands for animals. One group has successfully caught and decorated a horse. They look proudly towards another who has adorned the neck of a bull with a garland of flowers and playfully mounted him. She gestures with an arm raised in triumph as if to say how easy it is to tame the bull. But Europa is pathetically and ironically unaware that the bull is Jupiter, the king of the gods, in disguise. He has fallen in love with her and Cupid continues to be in charge as he guides the reins. The bull stares out with an evil glint in his eye as if to suggest his intentions to the viewer and the painting's dark tone points to an ominous future.

The Rape of Europa *by Bernardo Cavallini [courtesy National Museums Liverpool]*

***Orpheus and Eurydice*** [room 8, not illustrated] Eurydice died of a snake bite as she was trying to escape from an unwelcome suitor. Orpheus, who could charm anyone with his music, went down into the underworld to try to win his wife back. He even persuaded Hades, the god of the underworld, to release her but it was on condition that he should not look behind him as she followed him on the way back to the world above. At the last moment he could not resist looking round to see if she was behind him, and she vanished forever.

## Walker Art Gallery
Picture Gallery: Arion and the dolphin; Echo and Narcissus

*Arion saved by the dolphin* [room 8] Arion is riding a dolphin in triumph, accompanied by some Nereids and their offspring. He was skilled at playing the cithara, and his patron Periander, tyrant of Corinth in Greece, had allowed him to travel to Sicily to compete in a music festival, which he won. As he was sailing back laden with gifts after his victory, the sailors threatened to seize his goods and throw him overboard. Arion asked a favour to play for one last time, prayed to his father Neptune and sea nymph mother to help him, and jumped into the sea. Attracted by his magical playing a dolphin appeared, and here Arion is returning to Corinth mounted on the dolphin and giving thanks to the gods for his deliverance from death. Arion arrived back at Corinth before the sailors and told Periander what had happened. When the sailors reached port, they were summoned by him and, confronted by Arion, convicted on the spot. There are other ancient accounts – historical and mythical – about humans riding dolphins which may explain why they are represented as carrying Neptune, and his male and female companions, the Tritons and Nereids (see page 13 and CL22-7).

***Echo and Narcissus*** [room 8] Echo is in love with Narcissus, but he only with himself, infatuated with his own reflection in the pool. Unfortunately Echo cannot express her love as she can only repeat the last words spoken to her. This was the punishment Juno had given her for telling stories to distract her while Jupiter enjoyed himself with his favourite nymphs. The scene is beautiful but full of foreboding and the flowers at Narcissus' feet carry an ominous message. Echo will pine away with her unrequited love until only her voice remains. Narcissus too will waste away as his love will never be returned and when he dies the flower that bears his name will spring up in memory of him, tinged with the red of his blood.

Echo and Narcissus *by John William Waterhouse [courtesy National Museums Liverpool]*

*opposite:* Arion *by George Frederic Watts [courtesy National Museums Liverpool]*

***Mercury Stealing the Cattle of the Gods*** [room 8] Even as an infant Mercury, patron of commerce, was distinguished for his trickery, a characteristic attributed by many through the ages to merchants. The little boy Mercury can be recognised by his winged helmet which he will need when he grows up to be the messenger of the gods. He has stolen some cattle from Apollo and he also holds a stick that he has used to herd them, reminiscent of the caduceus which, with a snake, will form his emblem (see page 9 and CL 28-9). He meets an old man who rests his foot on his spade and leans on the handle to listen to him. By his gestures the impish rascal is letting him know where he has hidden the cattle and telling him to keep it a secret. But the old man sees the obvious, meets deceit with deceit, and looks at him seriously as he should. He wears a broad-brimmed hat, as Mercury would when he lays aside his winged helmet, and his spade is like Mercury's caduceus. It is as if an aged Mercury is observing his infancy. The idea for the picture came from Homer's *Hymn to Hermes*.

***Venus and Anchises*** [room 8, by William Blake Richmond, not illustrated] Venus has fallen in love with a shepherd Anchises and is visiting him on Mount Ida near Troy. He is in the shadows: she wishes to keep the assignation secret, as she is a goddess and he only a mortal. In her eagerness to reach her lover she is skipping over the flowers. They and the blossom herald the coming of Spring. Her doves of peace fly around: they and the lion and lioness that accompany her symbolise love as a great creative force in nature. Their son will be the great hero Aeneas who had special meaning for the Romans. After the sack of Troy, Aeneas sailed to Italy under divine guidance and his descendants Romulus and Remus founded Rome. Through them, Julius Caesar claimed descent from Venus, and his great nephew Augustus, the first Roman emperor, encouraged the Roman poet Virgil to write his epic poem the *Aeneid* about his famous ancestor (see pages 17 and 20).

*opposite:* Mercury stealing the Cattle of the Gods *by Edward John Poynter. The picture is framed by two finely wrought gilded Ionic columns. [courtesy National Museums Liverpool]*

Psyche in the Temple of Love *by Edward John Poynter [courtesy National Museums Liverpool]*

**Psyche in the Temple of Love** [room 8] *Psyche* is the Greek for soul and also butterfly, soul's symbol. Here, Psyche is gazing at a butterfly and dreaming, as if looking into her soul. Her beauty had incurred the jealousy of Venus who told her son Cupid to make Psyche fall in love with an ugly creature. But Cupid could not help falling in love with her himself. He brought her to a beautiful palace, where he visited her every night but never during the day. When she accidentally woke and recognised her lover, he deserted her and she went in search of him. Being advised that Venus would help, she went into her temple, the temple of love. As she dreams of her lover the doves of Venus hover ominously, hinting at the trials she was to be set by Venus. However, she overcame them with the help of friendly gods and goddesses, and appealed to Jupiter, king of the gods. He changed her into a goddess, thus facilitating her marriage to Cupid, and she bore a child Voluptas (Latin for desire).

**On the Terrace** [room 8, picture on page 58] Idly and dreamily the girl plays with a feather on a palm leaf. She, and everything around her, embody beauty, prosperity and peace. The scene presents an idealised picture of life in one of the most peaceful eras of the Roman empire around the bay of Naples. The balustrade is embellished with Classical patterning, and leads your gaze, and maybe her thoughts, to the sea and what it brings: boats bearing luxuries from overseas like the grapes – or lovers, the stuff of dreams. But this is calm before a titanic catastrophe (see below and the two contrasting pictures on pages 58-9).

**Faithful unto death** [room 8, picture on page 59] Disaster struck in AD 79 when the volcanic eruption of Mount Vesuvius covered Pompeii with ash to a depth of 15m. For centuries the town was hidden, then discoveries made that enabled artists to recreate the luxuries, but also the realities and tragedies of the disaster. The skeleton of a Roman soldier reminds you of the heroism and self-sacrifice that can arise at such a crisis. Our hero stands firm, gazing steadfastly at the advancing and all enveloping fire that gives the scene its reddish glow. In contrast, the figures behind are in turmoil or strewn on the floor. Others may flee but he stays faithfully at his post and this devotion to military duty was popular with the Victorians. It epitomises the security that it would create, safeguarding the prosperity that they would imagine enjoying *On the terrace*.

On the Terrace *by Edward John Poynter. Alma-Tadema later painted a series of views in the same vein, with aristocratic ladies and a dizzying perspective based on Pompeii. One of these,* Coign of Vantage, *for many his quintessential work, may owe its inspiration to this painting.*
*[courtesy National Museums Liverpool]*

Faithful unto death *by Edward John Poynter [courtesy National Museums Liverpool]*

**Helen of Troy** [go through room 7 to 6] Here is the *femme fatale* whose beauty was responsible for the fall of Troy (see page 40). Her long flowing hair and flowers – with roses symbolising love – represent a female beauty admired by the Victorians. But her attitude is one of moodiness, petulance and unconcern for any unhappiness she may cause. This Victorian interpretation of her appearance and character differs substantially from her original image portrayed in the works of Homer. There her beauty excelled all others; it attracted the admiration of the older generation as well as the desire of the younger; she was especially distinguished for her fine, long hair, lovely complexion and white arms. In character she was a dutiful housewife, consistently home loving with a talent for weaving. She was a sensitive

and perceptive hostess, aware of her guests' comforts and feelings, and generous in satisfying them. She had a particular talent for quick, effective and appropriate responses to tricky situations. She appreciated the goodness of others, expressing her admiration not only for her Greek husband Menelaus but also for Hector, her Trojan brother-in-law. After twenty years of marriage with Paris her ardour had cooled but she still loved him. She regretted her elopement with him, a moment of madness

which she blamed on the influence of Aphrodite. She still had a strong affection for her former husband Menelaus and wished to return home to him. Consequently she wanted the war to end any way it could and would do anything to help the Greeks to win. She was universally condemned, even hated, for being the cause of the conflict. Self-deprecating, she was conscious of this criticism, repented of her actions and wished she had never been born. However, the adverse reinterpretation of her character in later Greek literature is reflected in her portrayal here.

**Landscape with Phaeton's Petition to Apollo** [room 5] Phaeton continually plagued his father Apollo, the sun god, to let him drive his sun-chariot for the day. Apollo looks down on him, disdainfully playing his lyre. Phaeton is on his knees appealing to his mother and baby sister sitting on her mother's lap. They supported his unfortunate plea and Apollo finally relented. But Phaeton was unable to control the steeds, first driving them so high that everyone shivered and then so low that the crops were scorched. Jupiter, enraged, killed him with his thunderbolt and the bright dawn ended in sadness.

*above:* Landscape with Phaeton's Petition to Apollo *by Richard Wilson (detail). Apollo is portrayed as god of music on pages 87, 89, 117 and 126.* [courtesy National Museums Liverpool]

*opposite:* Helen of Troy *by Frederick Sandys* [courtesy National Museums Liverpool]

***View of the Ruins of Rome*** [room 5, opposite Phaeton's Petition]. Painted about 1741, this is an imaginary view with the ruins arranged and portrayed artistically, a picture postcard view of the city to be taken home by a tourist of the time. On the left are the Corinthian

columns of the temple of Hadrian which originally had 8 columns on its façade and 15 on each side. There appear to be 10 as painted so the artist has adapted the design to suit the view. To the right of this is the Pantheon whose dome exceeds that of St Peter's in diameter and whose columns are the same height as those of the temple of Hadrian, so the composition has lost the huge scale of the building. However, the artist has eliminated the unsightly bell towers added by Bernini in the 17th century, christened the asses' ears and pulled down in 1893, thus restoring the original appearance of the building. The obelisk is not the one that now stands in front of the Pantheon but in the Piazza del Popolo. Panini has left out the initial IMP (for imperator *emperor*) recording the action of the Roman emperor Augustus Caesar who brought the obelisk from Egypt to Rome in 10 BC (see page 100).

On the left of the right hand half of the picture is the triumphal arch of the Roman emperor Titus, erected to celebrate his capture of Jerusalem in 69 AD. Once again Panini seems to have improved the appearance of the arch, as a painting of Canaletto of the same period shows it in an extremely dilapidated condition. Subsequently stone facing has been restored to the upper storey. The temple with Ionic columns was dedicated to the god Portunus in 75 BC but used to be referred to as that of Fortuna Virilis (manly fortune). It is a good representation of how it looks even now, as also the column of Trajan. This was set up in 113 AD to celebrate his victory over the Dacians (modern Romania). It has a continuous frieze running round it depicting his campaigns, a most valuable source for Roman military practice. The statue of St Peter on the top replaces the original one of Trajan, lost in the middle ages.

*opposite and above: left and right hand halves of a* View of the Ruins of Rome *by Giovanni Paolo Panini (or Pannini) [courtesy National Museums Liverpool]*

## Walker Art Gallery
### Picture Gallery: Meleager and Atalanta

***Meleager and Atalanta*** [room 4] Feelings are not those we would expect from devoted hunters. He tenderly caresses her; she, demurely, seems unsure of accepting the honour and his love; she has to be encouraged by the gentle nudge of one of her hunting dogs; neither he nor she has a weapon and she is not dressed for the chase; the only reminder of the hunt is the horn, hung to rest. But all is not well: the winged boy Cupid, son of Venus, symbol and cause of love, is dipping his hands in the boar's blood and one of the Fates hovers ominously above. For when Meleager was only seven days old, they had announced that he could live only as long as one of the logs on the hearth remained unburned. His mother quickly snatched it away, and hid it in a chest. Now, her brothers, Meleager's uncles, will disagree because he has chosen to present the boar's head to Atalanta – his prize and passion – and a violent quarrel will ensue in which Meleager will kill them. His mother will then cast the fatal log she has so carefully saved into the fire.

*Apollo and Coronis* is just below *Meleager and Atalanta* (see page 47).

*above:* Meleager and Atalanta *from the studio of Paul Peter Rubens (detail on front cover)*
*right:* Atalanta and Meleager *by Charles le Brun. Note that Atalanta comes first in the title, not as is usual the other way round: all attention is on her in this depiction of the scene.*
*[both courtesy National Museums Liverpool]*

***Atalanta and Meleager*** [room 3] Meleager has triumphed in arms and love. A great band of heroes – and Atalanta – has gathered to hunt a wild boar. Meleager has killed the boar and presented its head to Atalanta, with whom he has fallen in love, because she has drawn first blood in the chase. Atalanta, seated on a tiger skin, the spoil of her hunting, is the focus of everyone's attention. Meleager has brought the boar's head in a bag and now brings it out, gazing at her intently as he awaits her response. *Her* attendant draws her – and our – attention to his approach, while *his* attendant looks at her, again drawing our look towards her. Atalanta's bow reminds us of the crucial part her wounding of the boar played in their relationship and present encounter, while Meleager's sword, used to sever the boar's head from its body, and now just withdrawn from its sheath in a gesture of readiness to venture all for her, is a presage of the catastrophic outcome. Significantly the spear, the weapon used to fight the boar, is held by his attendant. The dogs reflect their feelings: Meleager's hunting hound eagerly anticipating his master's wishes; Atalanta's house dogs, jumping down from the rug covering her lap, attentive but wary. The edge of her crimson canopy hovers uncertainly over and between them and she gestures tentatively. His fate is in her hands.

# Walker Art Gallery

## Picture Gallery: Diana and Endymion; Mercury and Juno; Pyramus and Thisbe

***Diana and Endymion*** [room 3] If you had any doubt what the mature woman's feelings are for the young man, look at Cupid with his sure and unmissable shot. The goddess Diana gazes with wrapt and wondering devotion at Endymion who is entirely oblivious of the passion he has aroused. He has laid aside his quiverful of arrows and his dogs are quiet: alert or sleeping. Ironically the arrows of the goddess of hunting are barely visible, slung unused on her shoulder, and the dogs that tore Actaeon to pieces are nowhere to be seen. Other cupids cavort in glee at the sport. However, while as goddess of chastity she will never consummate her love, as goddess of the moon her kiss will keep him in perpetual sleep where she can gaze at his eternal youth forever.

*above: Diana and Endymion by Francesco Solimena*
*opposite top:* Mercury and Juno *by Tacca*
*opposite bottom: Detail of* Landscape with Pyramus and Thisbe *by Gaspard Dughet [all courtesy National Museums Liverpool]*

**Mercury and Juno** When Jupiter fell in love with Semele and Bacchus was born, Juno, consumed by jealousy, tried to destroy the child but he was saved by Mercury. This statue may represent Mercury uncovering a jug from which to pour a libation to make peace with Juno.

**Landscape with Pyramus and Thisbe** [room 3] The beauty of the landscape belies the unfolding tragedy. Thisbe rushes distraught towards Pyramus who lies prostrate and dead on the ground. Living next door to each other, they had fallen in love but their parents forbade them to marry. Communicating with each other through a hole in a wall, they arranged to meet in a grove outside the city. Thisbe arrived first but was scared off by a lion which tore her shawl that slipped off as she fled. Pyramus arrived, saw the bloodstained shawl and killed himself, believing her to have been mauled to death by the lion. Now Thisbe too will kill herself and the tragedy will be complete.

***Landscape with Bacchus and Ceres*** [room 3] Liverpool does not appear to have publicly supported the activities of Bacchus (god of wine) – unsurprisingly, or Ceres (goddess of the harvest) – surprisingly. Here he is picking grapes as his contribution to the harvest while she, wreathed in cornflowers and holding a basket of bread, emerges from the stream after bathing, maybe to picnic on the bank. Her companion, preceding her, gives warning of Bacchus and of his companion, a Satyr, half man and half goat, and endowed with its lascivious nature. Fortunately, he is uninterested in the attractive females because he is asleep, presumably after overindulging himself as usual with wine. An assistant carries off a basket of grapes; he may or may not be a satyr as we cannot see his bottom half but satyrs are more likely to be at play rather than work (see page 88).

*Landscape with Bacchus and Ceres by Nicolas Poussin (detail). There is a most unusual female satyr portrayed on page 125. [courtesy National Museums Liverpool]*

***The Flight of Cloelia*** [room 3 not illustrated] shows the Roman heroine crossing the river Tiber as she leads her fellow hostages back to Rome (see page 71).

**Landscape with Ashes of Phocion** [room 3] Phocion's widow is secretly burying his ashes. She is intent lovingly on her task while her assistant looks round to see if they are being observed. But she need not worry: she is an insignificant figure amidst the busyness and unconcern of normal life. Ironically Phocion was an extremely significant figure in his time in ancient Athens and the idealised beauty of the Greek landscape masks an ugly history. Phocion 'The Good' (c402-318 BC) lived through a turbulent time in Greek politics that ended in the subjugation of Athens by Philip II of Macedon, Alexander the Great's father. Year on year he was democratically elected to the most important office of general – a record 45 times – but at the age of 84 he was illegally accused and condemned to death for treason when a Macedonian nominee was appointed to rule the city. He died taking hemlock (like Socrates), and under the terms of the execution was buried outside Athenian territory. However, his widow has secretly brought his ashes back to Athens and is burying them there. Soon the Athenians will repent of their injustice, rebury him at the public expense and execute his accuser.

*Detail of* Landscape with Ashes of Phocion *by Nicolas Poussin [courtesy National Museums Liverpool]*

*Detail (bottom left) of* The Triumph of Fortitude *by the School of Brussels [courtesy National Museums Liverpool]*

**The Triumph of Fortitude** [room 2] One of a series of tapestries depicting the four cardinal virtues and three theological ones (see page 14). The figure of Fortitudo (Latin for Fortitude) is prominent in the centre top of the tapestry and above it is a Latin elegiac couplet: *Obicit adversis interrita corda periclis/Virtus. eque iuvat morte recepta salus.* (Courage presents fearless hearts to adverse dangers. And winning salvation from death helps.)

The characters are a mix of Biblical and Classical examples. On the left of the detail illustrated are shown three legends from the early history of Rome when it was besieged by the Etruscan King Porsenna in 510 BC. Mucius Scaevola, sent by the Roman senate to assassinate the King but apprehended, was ordered to be burnt alive. He held his right hand in a fire to prove his endurance (hence his name Scaevola, *left-handed*; see the border of his robe) and was set free. Horatius Cocles held a bridge against the advancing Etruscans single-handedly while it was being demolished and leapt from it into the river Tiber to swim for safety when it fell. Cloelia was held as a hostage by the Etruscans but led her companions escaping to safety across the Tiber under a hail of missiles (see picture in room 3). Riding the two lions (symbols of Fortitude and pulling her chariot) are Dentatus who led the Romans to victory in the Samnite wars (3$^{rd}$ century BC) accompanied by Sinope, mythical queen of the Amazons. Penthesilea, another queen of the Amazons, is on the right with a spear so long it reaches the border. She was defeated by Achilles in battle who fell in love with her as she lay dying. Scaeva, shown pierced with spears, arrows and swords was a centurion in Julius Caesar's army. Caesar says his shield had at least 120 holes in it after a battle at Dyrrachium, but he survived. Other characters are mostly Biblical but Alexander the Great appears (very small) top left of the tapestry.

***Ulysses shooting through the rings*** [room 1, by Francesco Primaticcio, not illustrated. Ulysses is the Roman name for Odysseus]. Odysseus has spent twenty years away from home, ten fighting in the Trojan War (see pages 40-41) and another ten on his way home (the subject of Homer's epic poem *The Odyssey*). Now he reaches the ultimate test. In the meantime his palace has been taken over by suitors who have tried for years to persuade Odysseus' wife Penelope to give up hope for his return and marry one of them. Odysseus has now returned, disguised as a beggar. Penelope offers to marry whichever suitor passes a trial of strength and skill that Odysseus used to perform: to shoot an arrow through the sockets of twelve axe heads set in a row. Odysseus begs to be allowed to try first before the suitors. Now he is shooting to pass the test and will then throw off his disguise, shoot the suitors themselves and win Penelope back. The last line of Tennyson's poem *Ulysses* 'To strive, to seek, to find, and not to yield' was chosen to inspire athletes at the 2012 London Olympics.

# Central Library
## Picton Library

*Entrance 'doorways' in Erechtheion style [HH]*

The wooden panelling of the Picton Library is remarkable for its overall Classical design and exquisite detail. The circular construction is modelled on the British Museum reading room, in its turn modelled on the Pantheon with its dome. The two lower tiers are linked by superimposed Classical style pilasters in Roman Doric form (CL52-3). Appropriately each is adorned by a (single) triglyph with guttae (CL46). This pattern of decoration is repeated (in pairs) round the upper gallery precisely above their lower counterparts in an elongated form ending in a half scroll. Superimposed is a lintel patterned by simplified rosettes and, above that (reminiscent of a Greek temple), a form of pediment crowned by anthemions. These features serve to break up what would otherwise have been a continuous and monotonous length of shelves. Looking like entrance doorways in Erechtheion style, they are also designed to fit in with the entrance doorway which has a broader aspect (five rosettes in breadth instead of three on the pediment). The scrolls are decorated with triglyphs and guttae. Such is the extravagance of embellishment that was considered necessary to create the right atmosphere for learning, and could be afforded at the time.

*opposite (above): Picton Library overall design. The photograph was taken when the shelves had been cleared for refurbishment.*
*(below): Detail of Roman Doric with triglyphs and guttae [both HH]*

# Central Library
## Hornby Library

Leading off the Picton Library to the rear, the Hornby Library houses the city's collection of the rarest and most valuable books, maps and manuscripts. Like the Picton, although not on such a grand scale, it has Classical adornment lavished on it. The overall design of the library is barrel vaulted like the baths of Caracalla. Where one order is placed on top of another it is traditional for the lower order to be Doric, then Ionic, then Corinthian on top (CL54-5). Here, the gallery is supported at the end by pillars in Roman Doric style but the Ionic columns link the two storeys and support the roof. Peering out between the scrolls appear to be angels with wings. Above are extremely pronounced dentils with the ubiquitous ovolo (egg and dart) embellishment above that.

*Hornby Library interior [HH]*

*Ionic capitals with dentils and egg and dart embellishment (CL78-9)*
*[HH]*

# World Museum
## Statue of Athena

The World Museum is unique in Liverpool, containing as it does original works of Greek art, not just interpretations. It therefore gives us a valuable insight into the origins of the Classical forms we see today. However, modern works inspired by ancient originals must not be thought inferior as being mere copies or deviations. The Classical tradition was continually developing in ancient times as it still does now with artists adding their own individual version to the whole. There is thus no standard form for the depiction of the Greek gods and figures of myth and legend. However, the Greek vases in the World Museum are as close as we can get to the visual starting point and it is intensely interesting to observe how they were imagined in the early stages of the process.

At the entrance to the museum there is a Roman statue of Athena, inspired by the image that was worshipped in the Parthenon, her temple on the Acropolis in Athens (see pages 34-6 and CL30-1). This original statue was huge, held a statue of Victory 2m high in her hand and was chryselephantine (made of gold and ivory): the flesh parts and the head of Medusa on her aegis (tasselled martial cloak, CL33, 38) were made of ivory, her dress of gold. Here she holds an owl, the sign of her wisdom, but this and her right arm are later additions (see also pages 82 and CL30).

Athena is the Roman form of the Greek Athene. In view of the makers and subjects of the vases and statues in the Museum, in most cases the Greek names of the deities are used. See the appendix for Roman equivalents.

*Athena [HH]*

*All photographs taken in the World Museum (pages 77-101) are included courtesy of National Museums Liverpool (World Museum).*

## World Museum
Examination Hall mural

The coffee shop in the World Museum used to be the examination hall of the Central Municipal Technical School of Liverpool that opened in 1906. The mural by the serving counter has as its centrepiece the crowned figure of Liverpool who presides over the distribution of rewards to scholars (on the left) and industrial workers (on the right). The scholars exhibit a combination of desirable characteristics: (from the left) successful study as shown by the laurel wreath, enthusiasm for learning, modesty and respect, although this little figure holds a palm, which signifies victory or triumph (in later life?).

*Mural in the World Museum Hall (left hand half) [PO]*

The group of workers on the right include a blacksmith, a labourer and a man with a bale of cotton. They are headed by Mercury, the god of commerce, with his winged helmet and sandals (CL28-9) who lays an encouraging and congratulatory hand on the blacksmith's biceps. In giving them a laurel wreath for victory, Liverpool is assisted by Minerva, patroness of art and industry, recognisable by her shield decorated with the head of the Gorgon Medusa which refers to her other role as goddess of war (see page 100 and CL33). However, this is played down as most of the shield is hidden. Typical of the age (early 20th century) all the scholars and workmen are male (but those who give the rewards are female!)

*Mural in the World Museum Hall (right hand half) [PO]*

## World Museum
Entrance Hall murals and architecture (not open to the public)

In the passage leading from the old Byrom Street entrance to the old Examination Hall there are some more murals, one of which contains another figure of Minerva in the role of Liverpool (CL30-3). Recognisable by her helmet and aegis with the head of Medusa set in it, she encourages two figures with her staff, the female representing the arts and the male, industry. The border is a bay leaf garland (CL79, 85).

*Detail of mural in old Museum Entrance Hall [PO]*

The mural is supported by beautiful wooden panelling with Ionic columns and pediment framing the foundation stone of the *Technical School and Museum.*

*Panelling in old Museum Entrance Hall [PO]*

Roman Doric columns enhance the fireplace, the focal point of the entrance hall. Over the fireplace is a relief depicting putti who hold a shield emblazoned with a Liver Bird and below it a riband proclaiming Liverpool's Latin motto. A door to the right leads into the main hall.

*Columns and fireplace in Entrance Hall [PO]*

On a mural balancing the one on the opposite page Liverpool wears a crown like her namesake in the main hall. On her back she carries a bag containing fruit and grasps a medallion on which a Liver Bird is encircled by the Liverpool motto. To the left a small boy with cloth cap appears to be writing. He represents Mercury (CL28), god of commerce and trade, as can be seen by his caduceus half hidden behind him (see page 9). The unusual cap has a resemblance to Mercury's broad-brimmed hat (see page 55) but holds greater significance if you look to the figure on the right who is wearing the same. The meaning must be that the child who studies at the technical school will grow up to be someone who will play an important part in the commercial and industrial life of the city, and bring wealth and prosperity to it as personified by the other, winged, female figure carrying a basket laden with fruit. The connection is reinforced by the landscape in the background showing a ship in full sail and industrial buildings.

*Mural with Liverpool, two Mercuries and Prosperity [PO]*

## World Museum
Greek vases: Panathenaic amphorae

[Numbers in square brackets refer to the display cases in the Greek gallery, clockwise from the left as you enter.]

Despite the name, Greek vases were not just for decoration but also for use in storage, drinking, self-adornment and worship. Amphorae were most commonly used for storage and the sarcophagus of a baker in the Roman gallery shows how they were used (see opposite). The most decorative of these were Panathenaic vases, given to the thousand winners in the festival of that name which was held every four years at Athens. Athene appears on one side of the vase and a representation of the event on the other. Although the form of the vase is that of an amphora it is likely that the vases were in most cases kept for show and taken by the winners to their grave. This may be why so few have surfaced in excavations. However, they have been discovered throughout the Greek world and beyond, so it seems that many winners may have cashed in on their success. Athene may be accompanied by an owl, symbol of her wisdom.

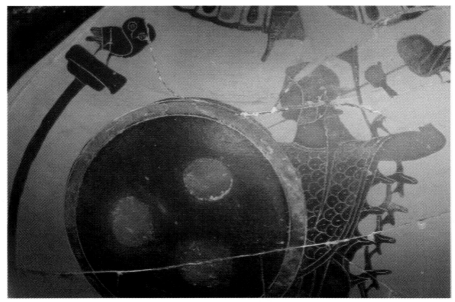

*Athene and owl* [3] *[PO]*

*Detail of a baker's sarcophagus showing amphorae being used. At the bottom an amphora is being filled and at the top being carried away empty from a huge storage vessel. The pointed ends were particularly useful for stowing away in ships where they could be inserted into grooves and prevent slippage* [Roman gallery] *[PO]*

## World Museum
### Greek vases: Athene; Gorgons

In addition to her role in arts and crafts, Athene was goddess of war. In the picture opposite, Athene is shown in a warlike pose, accompanied by a cock who may symbolise her – and the winner's – competitive and combative spirit. She wears her trademark helmet and tasselled war cloak (aegis), symbolising a Gorgon's hair of snakes, but it does not carry the terrifying image of the head of the Gorgon Medusa (see detail on crater vase below, pages 79 and 100, and CL33, 38). On other vases her shield may sport a snake, or a triple symbol, most spectacularly a three-legged man, later adopted by the Isle of Man [4]. This may point to a connection with Hecate, the goddess of the three ways or cross roads.

*Gorgon heads on a vase of a much later style, manufactured in southern Italy [2] [PO]*

*Athene and cock* [3] *[PO]*

# World Museum
Greek vases: hydria; Athenian deities; black and red figure vases

Wine was stored in amphorae, but water would be carried from the source and kept in a hydria, which has handles for lifting and pouring. The figures on the hydria opposite [6] are identifiable by their attributes. From left to right: Dionysus holds a kantharos (a drinking cup with high handles) a type of vessel often associated with him; Athene wears her aegis, a cloak tasselled with a fringe of snakes, and a helmet with a preposterous plume that has to break the frame so that she may be the same size as the other deities; Apollo plays the lyre; Artemis is nuzzled by a deer and accompanies her brother's music with a castanet. The picture of the four gods at leisure is reminiscent of the similar picture on the Parthenon frieze (see page 35). As the Athenians came to dominate the production of pottery, it is not surprising that Athene is the most popular representation of the deities. However, other gods are well represented: Dionysus because of his association with drinking, and Apollo and Artemis because of their interests in music and hunting. Hermes commonly attends other deities but Poseidon, in spite of the Athenians' success as seafarers, is conspicuously absent, maybe because he was responsible for storms and he competed unsuccessfully with Athene for possession of Attica, the area round Athens (see inside front cover).

Illustrated so far have been some *black figure* vases produced by painting the figures in black slip on top of the natural red of the clay. These were superseded by *red figure* vases as in examples on the following pages, where the whole surface was covered in black slip which was then removed to reveal the image in red. This gave a more natural look and enabled the potter to paint finer and more expressive detail on the figures.

*opposite: Hydria with (left to right) Dionysus, Athene, Apollo and Artemis [6] [PO]*

Wine from an amphora and water from a hydria were poured into a crater or mixing bowl before being drunk at a party. The amount of dilution was dictated by someone appointed to regulate the tempo of the festivities (see page 21). On the crater illustrated [1] Zeus, a commanding figure who endorses this scene of festivity, brandishes his thunderbolt. An effeminate Apollo plays his cithara, a form of lyre, to provide the music; wine is suggested by Dionysus who holds his thyrsus, a staff topped with a pine cone and decorated with vine and ivy leaves. Joining in is a satyr, a hard drinking worshipper of Dionysus with typical receding hair, budding horns, and the ears, tail and lascivious nature of a goat (see page 68). The festive scene is framed by women worshippers, one of them dancing and maybe hinting at the legend horrifically dramatised in Euripides' play *The Bacchae* (worshippers of Bacchus, i.e. Dionysus) where the revelling Agave with her companions tears her unbelieving son to pieces in her frenzy. So maybe the outward joy is, like life, tinged with an inner sadness.

The Panathenaic amphorae (see page 82) were filled with oil: a valuable prize as well as a trophy. When the oil was to be used by athletes they would decant the oil from the storage amphora to a smaller container called a lekythos which could be carried around by an athlete to anoint himself when required. This had a narrow neck so that the valuable oil would not gush out and be wasted. It might also be placed on a grave with an offering of oil to the gods, in which case it might have a false neck to give the impression of a full container and avoid wasting precious oil (see pages 90-1).

*above: Crater with Zeus, Apollo, Dionysus and companions* [1]

*opposite: Athenian gravestone* [1] *(see commentary on page 128)*
*[both PO}*

On this lekythos (see page 88) Apollo and Artemis are pouring libations from a container called a phiale. On one side Apollo may be identified by his lyre, his youthful appearance and luxuriant hair.

*Apollo* [1] *[PO]*

On the other side his sister is attended as usual by an animal, in this case a deer. On another lekythos the figure of Nike (Victory) is shown wearing wings as she usually does. There is however a temple on the Acropolis in Athens dedicated to Wingless Victory as the Athenians hoped that she would then never fly away from Athens! The lines of her dress and body underneath are finely delineated, showing the skill of the painter in using the red figure technique. She demonstrates the final stages of drinking or pouring out wine in a libation or offering to the gods. To do this she is holding a wine jug (oinochoe, 'wine pourer') in one hand which she would have dipped into a mixing bowl or crater to collect the wine, then transferred it to a phiale (a flat dish) in her other hand to make the libation over the altar. At a party the oinochoe was used to decant the diluted wine from the crater into a cup for drinking, as described and illustrated on page 21.

*Nike* [1] *[PO]*

Another amphora shows Heracles (Hercules for the Romans) fighting the Nemean lion. Heracles, the son of Zeus and Alcmena, was sent mad by the jealous Hera and killed his wife and children. For this he was condemned to carry out twelve labours set by his weakling cousin. The first one was to kill the Nemean lion (i.e. living in Nemea) that had an impenetrable skin. The muscularity of Heracles' thighs is notable and he is using his club (a stripped tree trunk) to batter the lion before realising this was useless – he had brain as well as brawn – and closing in to throttle it. He then used its razor-sharp claws to cut off its pelt and thereafter wore it as impenetrable armour (as shown in the pillars of St George's Hall underneath the organ, see page 22).

*left: Heracles fighting the Nemean lion* [1]
*[PO]*

In complete contrast to Heracles is a much later portrayal of Aphrodite's son Eros, god of love. He is usually personified as a young, pretty boy who playfully makes you fall in love by shooting with bow and arrow. Here he is portrayed as more mature (see page 36) with wings as usual but holding a patera (a dish for offerings to the gods, the same as a phiale – see page 91 – but as the vase was made in southern Italy the Latin word is used). It is a good example of the variety of representation and inventiveness characteristic of the treasure trove of Greek vases that always challenges our imagination.

*left: Eros [2] [PO]*

*Apollo Sauroktonos* (Apollo the lizard killer) shows Apollo as a young man trying to spear a lizard with a dart. The original was made about 350 BC by the Greek sculptor Praxiteles who came at the end of a long line of distinguished Greek sculptors of the Classical period. They had refined their skills over two centuries and Praxiteles developed the technique of contrapposto ('opposite') to give a more natural pose to a human figure. This is where hips and shoulders slant in opposite directions because of the movement of arms or legs (in this instance throwing the dart) and shifting the weight onto one foot. Praxiteles gave a more natural look to his statues by incorporating trees as an integral part of the composition to give support to the figure and its limbs, and is said to have employed a painter to colour his statues (see also pages 40-1). This is a Roman copy of the bronze original statue which, like most of the finest sculptures of antiquity, has been lost, but there is another copy of the statue in the Louvre which has a close resemblance to it. However, the minor differences of detail show that they are not exact copies of the original – which it would be difficult to reproduce exactly, particularly in sculpture.

*opposite: Apollo Sauroktonos* [between 4 & 5] *[PO]*

**Zeus** is readily identifiable through the eagle and his beard which represents him as a mature man, 'Father of the Gods'. The pose seems to indicate that he may be brandishing his thunderbolt, his main attribute, with which he may destroy enemies or wrong doers. Originally the sky god, he is imagined as venting his rage through lightning that accompanies thunder.

*Zeus* [between 6 and 1]
*[PO]*

*Artemis* the huntress can immediately be identified through her bow and arrow. She appears to be holding up her catch. She wears a short tunic or chiton that women wore for running – including their events at the Olympic games where the men competed naked. Women were normally portrayed with legs covered, except in erotic scenes. They were not depicted in the nude until late on in the development of Greek sculpture – Praxiteles was the first to do so with his sensational Aphrodite of Cnidos – but before his time sculptors and painters had perfected the art of revealing the female form underneath clothing, as this small statue shows (compare the size of the vase).

*Artemis* [1] *[PO]*

**Theseus** is the Athenian Heracles, wearing a distinctive Athenian helmet with elevated crest. He set himself labours to save the world from those who preyed on passers by, punishing them in the same way as they had treated their victims. Like his cousin Heracles, he gained his main weapon, a club, from his first conquest, but already made of bronze. He also used a sword, an heirloom, which he had retrieved from underneath a stone to prove his manhood. The weapons are cleverly designed to support his arms but the sculptor has chosen to portray him as a serene commander rather than a man of action, so the pose lacks movement compared with Praxiteles' Apollo (see page 95). Theseus inaugurated the Panathenaic festival (see page 82) extending an existing Athenian one to Attica, the area around Athens. It was at Theseus' wedding that the battle of the Lapiths and Centaurs took place (see page 37).

We cannot tell whether the Roman copyist of the Theseus statue took the pose from the Greek original or imposed it. The pose certainly is a typical Roman one as the statues of Augustus and the unknown senator show (see pages 100-101).

*opposite: Theseus* [between 4 & 5] *[PO]*

## World Museum
### Roman sculpture: Augustus; the toga

*Augustus*, the first Roman emperor, ended a period of bitter civil war (CL6) and wished to portray himself as a successful general and peaceful leader. Hence he bears the toga worn by Romans on civic occasions on his left arm and on his right military dress. This is reinforced by the breastplate emblazoned with a delightful decorative Gorgon's head, the hallmark of Minerva's armour (CL30) which also suggests divine ancestry. Augustus encouraged a cult of emperor worship, particularly in the eastern half of the Roman empire where this had been practised since the time of Alexander the Great. Such statues were set up throughout the empire to encourage the custom.

*left: Augustus [Roman gallery]*
*above: An ugly Gorgon, not fit for Augustus's breastplate! [6] (see also page 84)*
*[both PO]*

An unknown Roman man wears the formal attire of a Roman. The toga looked distinguished, but was in fact cumbersome and extremely unsuitable for most activities. Although the right arm was free, the left was encumbered and any quick and sudden movement would be difficult. The toga was used in commemorative statues until the early part of the nineteenth century, as for George Stephenson and William Roscoe in St George's Hall (see page 23), but was then superseded by Victorian dress.

*right: Unknown Roman man. It was common for bodies to be manufactured en masse and offered on spec with heads affixed when required, or even changed.* [Roman gallery] [PO]

Look at the baker's sarcophagus and commentary on page 83.

# Mersey Docks and Harbour Board Building
Pantheon; coats of arms

The magnificent stained glass windows are dedicated to some of the countries of the British Empire, a clarion roll call of its extent at the start of the 20th century. The Dominion of Canada and Union of South Africa sport coats of arms with Latin mottoes:

- Canada: *a mari usque ad mare* 'right from sea to sea'
- South Africa: *ex unitate vires* 'unity from strength'.

Colonies and protectorates have a standard design and may have a Latin motto:

- Gibraltar: *montis insignia Calpe* 'the badge of the rock of Gibraltar'
- Jamaica: *indus uterqve serviet uni* 'both Indians will serve one' (with reference to the collective servitude of the Taino and Arawak Indians to the colonisers)
- British Guiana: *damus petimusque vicissim* 'we give and take in turn' (this also appears on the world's rarest stamp).

The patterning on the dome is modelled on that of the Pantheon in Rome and the vaulted ceilings in the side aisles maybe on those used in the Baths of Caracalla in Rome (see page 110).

*'Pantheon' dome [PO]*

*left: The coat of arms of British Guiana [HH]*

*below left: Mersey Docks and Harbour Board coat of arms Below right: Standard bay leaf border for coats of arms. [both PO]*

# Mersey Docks and Harbour Board Building
## Baroque architecture

The interior of the Mersey Docks and Harbour Board Building is, like the exterior, a feast of baroque exuberance. Corinthian, the most decorative of the Greek orders of architecture, is the favourite form: not in traditional style but in exaggerated variation, as the accompanying illustrations show (CL50-1, 62-3).

*above: Elaborate Composite capitals with dentil decoration*

*left: Detail of above [both PO]*

*Elaborate in front and simple beyond, like the Liver Building (see page 108), with part of the full quotation from Psalm 107 that encircles the interior* They that go down to the sea in ships and do business in great waters *(see also page 102). The stained glass windows are behind. [PO]*

## Cunard Building
### Classical and Egyptian decoration; Board Room

How many passengers looked up and appreciated the intricate decorative detail of the main hall? With a mix of Classical and Egyptian styles – to hint at exotic foreign destinations? - the capitals of the squared columns have scrolls reminiscent of the Ionic order (CL48-9), and around the C for Cunard are flowers that could be Egyptian lotuses which also appear on the Roman Doric variation (CL53). Adjacent, on the ceiling are palmettes, and dentil and ovolo decoration (CL78-9) . Guttae appear in two forms: in rows of six on the vertical surfaces, as underneath the triglyphs of a Doric frieze, and also in panels on the underside of the ceiling in rows of 4x3 (instead of the more usual 6x3) to create the right proportions (CL46). Upstairs there are panels in the office doorways with coat of arms and an arresting Latin motto, and in the Board Room – how many saw this?! - exquisite carved wooden panelling with Classical influences in the ceiling.

*Main Hall: left: 'Ionic' capital and palmette*
*right: Guttae, and dentil and ovolo decoration [PO]*

below: The Board Room ceiling is decorated with Classical designs in the Wedgewood style that drew its inspiration from the discoveries made at Pompeii, accompanied by Egyptian sphinxes.

above: Classical embellishment in the wooden panelling of the Board Room: acanthus (like the Corinthian order, CL50-1) embracing rosettes with wheat sheaves bound like fasces, palmettes above and dentils overall (CL16-7, 78-9)

left: Office doorway panel: Fortis qui prudens 'brave [is the man] who [is also] sensible'

*[all on this page HH]*

# Liver Building
## modernist and stripped Classicism

Only five years separate the construction of the Mersey Docks and Harbour Board Building and the Liver Building but – to look at the interiors – it might be two hundred. We have leapt from the Baroque of the 17$^{th}$ century (CL62-3) almost to the modernist and stripped Classicism of the mid 20$^{th}$ century (CL68-71). Although in the entrance hall some decorative capitals and a Liver Bird add interest, in the main hall the capitals and scroll roof supports are extremely plain in colour and outline. On a much smaller scale, an egg and dart (ovolo) border does embellish the post boxes.

*Entrance Hall: Liver Bird and stripped capital [PO]*

*Main Hall: stripped capital and roof supports [PO]*

*left: Post box with egg and dart (ovolo) border*
*right: detail of border [PO]*

# India Buildings
vault ceilings and the baths of Caracalla

The colonnade more than any other in Liverpool gives you an idea of the scale of the baths of the emperor Caracalla in Rome. They were constructed on a huge scale (up to 35m in height), twice that of the India Buildings colonnade, the height of one of the side aisles of the

baths. The ceiling is decorated, like many concrete vaults in ancient Rome, with recessed patterning or coffers to make the roof lighter and decorate what would otherwise be a flat, drab surface. Such techniques were employed in the vast Caracalla baths complex (total area 27 acres, about 15 football pitches), capable of holding 1,600 people at the same time; the remains are now used for opera performances. The spendthrift emperor Caracalla ruled from 211-217 AD and gave Roman citizenship to all freeborn inhabitants of the Roman empire, who were thereby liable to taxation and will have contributed to the cost of his public works in the capital. Other Classical embellishments include Ionic columns (CL48-9), guilloche patterning to decorate the vaulted archways (CL79) and staircase pillars which incorporate a column in the Roman Doric order (CL52-3).

*India Buildings: opposite above: Staircase pillar; opposite below: Ionic capital and guilloche patterning; above: Ceiling [all HH]*

## Town Hall
Pantheon; Liverpool motto

At the top the dome is decorated in the Pantheon style with the Liverpool motto in a band at the bottom. Between is a repeat design resembling the symbols of Mercury (caduceus, helmet and wings). Corinthian columns adorn the entrance hall.

*Interior of Town Hall dome [HH]*

## Martins Bank
### Side Entrance lobby

Liverpool's wealth came from the sea. This is the theme of the sculptural embellishment on the outside of Martins Bank, and it is reflected on the inside. In the side entrance lobby putti process holding cornucopias (CL18-9), filled with coins instead of the fruit and flowers of antiquity. The ceiling is decorated in the coffer pattern of the Pantheon with rosettes in the centre. A dentil frieze runs round below and the capitals of the columns are a variation of the Ionic with the scrolls transforming into palmettes, themselves forming a lapholder for fruit.

*Side Entrance lobby ceiling and capitals [HH]*

*M for Martins Bank [HH]*

The M symbols of Martins Bank support a cornucopia of coins, held up by what appear to be Classical columns but on closer inspection are like rods bound together with ropes, a motif of strength produced by smaller parts working closely together. They have their antecedents in the motto of the Union Bank of Liverpool (CL8-9) and look like the Roman fasces (rods and axes bound together as a symbol of authority, CL16-7). However too close a resemblance would have been politically unwise in view of the rise of fascism in the 1930s.

*top to bottom: Putti processing, Deposits, Loans [HH]*

The frieze portrays putti processing on one side towards a coffer indicating deposits and on the other away from the coffer indicating loans.

The main hall has fine columns in Classical style.

# Martins Bank
## Board Rooms

*Ionic capital [HH]*

Classical references to the overall wealth from the sea theme abound in the Board Room in lavish display on the eighth floor where there are beautifully wrought capitals on Ionic columns (CL48-9).

One mantelpiece fancifully portrays Nereids (CL24-5) being borne along by dolphins towards a coffer (Martins Bank) overflowing with coins. They approach from each side, the first two with tridents as a vanguard, the third (and we are to imagine many others) holding a cornucopia (CL18-9) filled with the fruits of overseas trade. The clock above has Egyptian style rope decoration.

*Nereid mantelpiece [HH]*

Midas who turned all to gold (CL38) appears on another mantelpiece appropriately appearing himself on a gold coin.

*Midas [HH]*

*Board Room lunettes (above) and detail (below) [HH]*

The lunettes above the wood panelling are an intricate mix of Classical and Egyptian. The arc surrounding the design is composed of strands bound together in the way that fasces were (see pages 112-3), depicting strength through unity. It also has reminiscences of the bay leaf garland design (see CL79). Dominating the centre of the design is a wonderfully imaginative Liver Bird, which together with the grasshopper represents the wealth of Liverpool – and Martins Bank.

Diminutive Ionic capitals enhance the coat of arms of Martins Bank at the bottom. On each side sea creatures support an Ionic column out of which emerges a trident, symbolic of Neptune, god of the sea, and therefore complete the design. The cornice is supported by double scrolls reminiscent of Greek Erechtheion style volutes (CL80) which are decorated with Egyptian patterning.

# Athenaeum
## Athene and Arachne; Apollo and Marsyas

The Athenaeum library is furnished in fine Classical style panelled in green with matching Doric columns stretching to the ceiling. As an integral part of the book cases there are three paintings by Edward Halliday commissioned in 1928 to illustrate Athene's life and works (CL30-1). Two are reproduced here and the third inside the front cover.

In weaving, Arachne boasted, she was the equal of Athene, goddess of craft. The picture below shows the result of her pride (*hybris* for the Greek writers of tragedy). Athene appears as an old woman (right) and throws off her disguise (centre foreground). Arachne (centre) defiantly challenges her to a contest. Athene weaves the story of her triumph over Poseidon (left foreground) and strikes Arachne with her own shuttle (left centre) as she slumps over her own inferior work. Terrified, Arachne rushes to the ladder leading up the scaffolding (rear right) and hangs herself. As she changes into a spider (hence the *arachnid* family) the shadow of her metamorphosing body is projected by the sunlight onto the opposite wall (rear left).

Athene was also involved in the tragic *hybris* of Marsyas. In the picture below she tries playing a flute made out of stag's bones but was dismayed to see her swollen cheeks reflected in a stream (top left). She throws it down with a curse on whoever plays it. Marsyas picks it up and charms some country girls (top right). They say that he surpasses Apollo who challenges him to a contest. Apollo (centre) wins with his lyre (see page 33) while Marsyas (in the foreground) throws his pipes away as he loses. Death (centre right) stands behind Apollo to punish the loser holding the knife he will use to flay him alive.

*opposite: Arachne and Athene by Edward Halliday reproduced with the kind permission of the Athenaeum. The artist has shown himself on the right looking at his own design being woven by Athene! (see his original picture used for this design inside the front cover.) [PO]*

*above:* Marsyas' contest with Apollo *by Edward Halliday reproduced with the kind permission of the Athenaeum. [PO]*

# The Vines
## Pan; putti; Caryatids; signs of the zodiac

The Vines Hotel has magnificent wood panelling in Classical style that rivals Martins Bank Board Room and is much more accessible. Above it is a plaster frieze with putti involved in various activities. The theme of the panel illustrated below is music and drama where three of them are decorating a statue of Pan holding his pipes, and another one is looking at a mask (see pages 122 and 127).

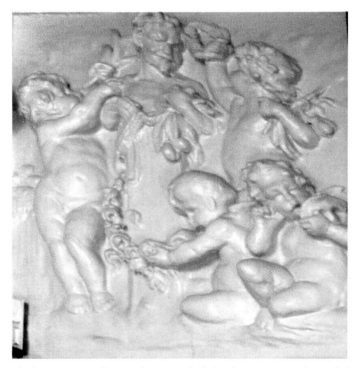

*left: putti on frieze: bottom left looking at mask and decorating Pan in the centre [HH]*

*right: Caryatid by fireplace [HH]*

The Adelphi Hotel opposite The Vines has fine interior columns in the New Classical style like the exterior. (CL66-7).

*Fireplace showing octagonal columns, small scrolls 'supporting' the lintel and gigantic ones framing the plaster panel above. This forms part of a frieze that continues (with repeats) right round the room. The panel illustrated opposite is in the corner (top left of the photo). Above that is Scorpio, one of the twelve signs of the zodiac portrayed on a decorative circular band on the ceiling. [HH]*

# Medical Institution
## Hippocrates

The floor of the old entrance hall to the Liverpool Medical Institution is adorned with a beautiful mosaic design. The Greek inscriptions embody some aphorisms or maxims of Hippocrates, a Greek doctor who lived in the 5th century BC. These are the ones that appear at the very start of his list, so would seem to be the most important for him as a doctor. They would also apply extremely effectively as a guide to practical life.

Illustrated opposite and reading clockwise from top left and then across the centre, they are transliterated into Roman characters and translated as follows:

O BIOS BRACHUS: life is short

E TECHNE MAKRE: skill is long (i.e. learning a skill is a lengthy process)

O KAIROS OXUS: opportunity is fleeting

E PEIRA SPHALERE: (making an) experiment is risky

E KRISIS CHALEPE: judgement is difficult

In the centre is the emblem of Asclepius the Greek god of medicine (see page 46). Its origins are obscure but the snake may represent the new life that healing brings, as the snake sloughs off its old skin. The staff may be a symbol of authority (like sceptre) or the magical effect of a cure (like a wand). Mercury has the same symbol (see page 9).

Hippocrates formulated the Hippocratic oath to which doctors used to subscribe, but now only in modified form. The reason for this will be apparent from some of the following extracts from the original:

- I will apply dietetic measures for the benefit of the sick according to my ability and judgment; I will keep them from harm and injustice.

- I will neither give a deadly drug to anybody if asked for it, nor will I make a suggestion to this effect. Similarly I will not give to a woman an abortive remedy.

- I will not use the knife, not even on sufferers from stone, but will withdraw in favour of such men as are engaged in this work.

- Whatever houses I may visit, I will come for the benefit of the sick, remaining free of all intentional injustice, of all mischief and in particular of sexual relations with both female and male persons, be they free or slaves.

- What I may see or hear in the course of treatment or even outside of the treatment in regard to the life of men, which on no account one must spread abroad, I will keep myself holding such things shameful to be spoken about.

*The aphorisms of Hippocrates [HH]*

# Philharmonic Hotel
## Apollo; fauns

Enter the hotel through the doorway decorated in gold above with the Latin motto *pacem amo 'I love peace'* (CL4, 11). On the right is the Grande Lounge beautifully panelled in wood with bronze reliefs. The fireplace is framed by a beautifully carved and detailed pair of Ionic columns. Over the doorway is a relief of Apollo being crowned with, appropriately, a laurel wreath which was used to honour victors at ancient Greek music festivals. On either side of the statuary are terms in the shape of fauns with pan pipes hanging down from their waists and cloven hoofs emerging from the bottom of the console brackets. Fauns are men with goat legs, followers of the Roman god Faunus who was identified with the Greek god Pan (see pages 118 and 127). There was also a Roman female equivalent Fauna. It is tempting to imagine that she or her followers are depicted in the consoles opposite with their cloven hoofs, maybe through modesty, covered by their long dresses but they are probably Nereids with fish tails instead of legs.

*Ionic column [PO]*

*Apollo and fauns [PO]*

*Nereids [PO]*

# Philharmonic Hall
## Stripped Classicism; musical moods

But is it Classicism stripped to the very minimum or is it in the imagination of the eye of the beholder (CL70-1)? Two rings at the top of the columns in the entrance hall can remind you of the three rings (anuli) at the top of a Doric column (CL47). Inside the auditorium, the decorated bands at the top of the columns in the boxes bear faint resemblances to those of the Ionic or Roman Doric order (CL48, 53), and the patterning repeated above (as in the Ionic order) to an extended repeated triglyph (polyglyph?) or echo of fluting on Greek columns.

*Anuli? (left) and Classical patterning? (right) [PO]*

Inside the auditorium, the six nude figures that grace the walls are often likened to the Greek muses, but there are only six instead of nine. In fact the designer, Edmund C Thompson said that they depicted different 'musical moods'. However, the middle two on each side certainly have Classical ancestry. The middle figure, on the right as you face the stage, is a Bacchante, a female follower of Bacchus (Dionysus) the god of wine whose worship invited orgiastic dancing (see page 88). The other, on the left, is a great rarity: a *female* satyr, whereas usually satyrs are raunchy males (see page 68) with an appetite for wine and women. She plays the pipes that are associated with Pan (see pages 117 and 123) and waves a thyrsus, a staff tipped by a pine cone, also used by Bacchantes and decorated with vine leaves.

*Female satyr (left) and Bacchante (right) [PO]*

# Philharmonic Hall
## Apollo and Pan

In the Grand Foyer Bar are two plaster and gold-leaf panels on a musical theme. One shows Apollo enchanting the world, including animals, with his music (like Orpheus, see page 51, who could also command the attention of trees).

The other shows Apollo being instructed by Pan. Amusingly, Apollo is being taught to play Pan's pipes and Pan is conducting him with a twig that he uses as a baton with the appropriate gestures with his other hand.

*opposite: Apollo enchanting the world, and below: Apollo being instructed by Pan [PO]*

# Oratory
## gravestones

Many of the memorials in the Oratory are modelled on ancient Greek gravestones (or stelai). There is one original stele in the Greek gallery of the World Museum (illustrated on page 88). The design is of the simplest: an unadorned seated figure (which is most economical of space), at rest, with a gesture that suggests us to be free from care too.

*Mary Robinson's gravestone*
*[PO]*

The features could be of anyone, and maybe that is how they were made, and chosen, by the deceased's family. Other, later, and more expensive, examples show extra decoration, more detailed clothing and more expressive emotion with the possible addition of another comforting person, who is also being comforted. Apart from the additional person, Mary Robinson's gravestone in the Oratory exhibits all these features. It is surmounted by a palmette for decoration (see CL44, 78) and she is seated, as befits a free lady of distinction. In this adaptation an oil lamp of ancient Greek design on a pillar maybe represents the extinguishing of the flame of life. As in ancient examples the figure is shown in relief and in profile to match the chair. A footstool gives distinction and ease to the deceased who is clad in traditional ancient Greek dress of peplos or long robe, its folds making a beautiful pattern, which delighted the Greeks.

# Appendix
## Greek and Roman gods

| Greek name | Roman name | Interests | Attributes |
|---|---|---|---|
| *Aphrodite | Venus | Love | Dove |
| *Apollo | Apollo (Phoebus) | Sun, music, medicine, prophecy, youth | Lyre |
| *Ares | Mars | War | |
| *Artemis | Diana | Moon, hunting | Animals, especially deer |
| Aesculapius | Asclepius | Healing | Staff with encircling serpents |
| *Athene | Minerva, Athena | Wisdom, crafts, war | Owl, cock, helmet, tasselled cloak |
| *Demeter | Ceres | Agriculture | |
| *Dionysus | Bacchus | Wine, poetry, drama | Thyrsus (rod tipped with a pine cone and encircled with vines or ivy) |
| Eros | Cupid | Love | Bow and arrow |
| Hades | Pluto | Underworld | |
| *Hephaestus | Vulcan | Fire, metalwork | |
| *Hera | Juno | Queen of gods, women, marriage, childbirth | |
| *Hermes | Mercury | Luck, wealth, merchants, thieves | Caduceus (staff with encircling serpents) |
| *Poseidon | Neptune | Sea | Trident |
| *Zeus | Jupiter | King of the gods, sky, justice | Thunderbolt, eagle |

*These together form the Twelve Olympians who lived on Mount Olympus in northern Greece. Olympia, home of the Olympic games is in southern Greece and is named after the patron god of the games, Olympian Zeus.

# Bibliography

Baulier, Francis *Hachette World Guide*: Greece (Hachette 1955)

Boardman, John *Athenian Black Figure Vases* (Thames and Hudson 1974)

Boardman, John *Athenian Red Figure Vases The Classical Period* (Thames and Hudson 1989)

Boardman, John and Griffin, Jasper and Murray, Oswyn *The Oxford History of the Classical World* (OUP 1986)

Cavanagh, Terry *Public Sculpture of Liverpool* (Liverpool University Press 1997)

Corbett, PE *The Sculpture of the Parthenon* (Penguin 1959)

Compton, Ann *Edward Halliday: Art for Life* (University of Liverpool Art Gallery 1997)

Fletcher, Sir Banister *A History of Architecture* (University of London 1961 and Architectural Press 1996)

Graves, Robert *The Greek Myths* (Penguin 1955)

Hollinghurst, Hugh *Classical Liverpool: language, sculpture and architecture* (Liverpool History Society 2008)

Hollinghurst, Hugh *John Foster and Sons: Kings of Georgian Liverpool* (Liverpool History Society 2009)

Knowles, Lorraine *St George's Hall Liverpool* (National Museums and Galleries on Merseyside 1988)

*Lexicon Iconographicum Mythologiae Classicae* (Artemis 1981)

Muirhead, L Russell *Rome and Central Italy* (Ernest Benn 1956)

Osborne, Robert *Archaic and Classical Greek Art* (OUP 1998)

Pausanias *Guide to Greece* (Penguin 1985)

Williams, Dyfri *Greek Vases British Museum* (British Museum Publications 1985)

Woodford, Susan *An Introduction to Greek Art* (Duckworth)

# Index

Illustrations are in **bold** type; Greek or Roman equivalents are in [square brackets].